Shape, Space and Measures

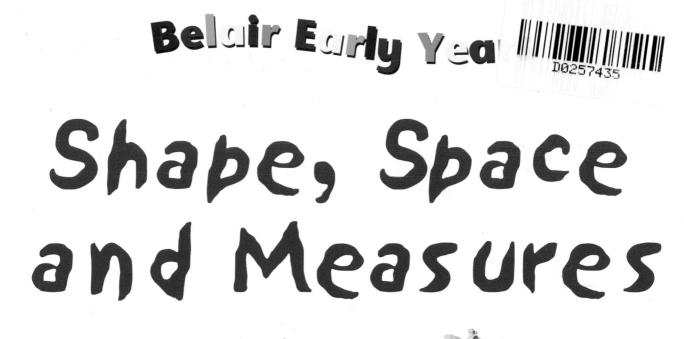

Bugs Alive

Katharine Newall

Acknowledgements

The author and publishers would like to thank the staff and children of Cliffe (VC) Primary School, Fishergate Early Years Unit and Selby Community Primary School for their flexibility and assistance in the production of this book. Special thanks also to my father Ray, for helping to set up some of the activities.

The author would like to dedicate this book to the memory of Sean Gooch, a generous man, an inspirational teacher and a great friend. I'm sorry you will never see my first book.

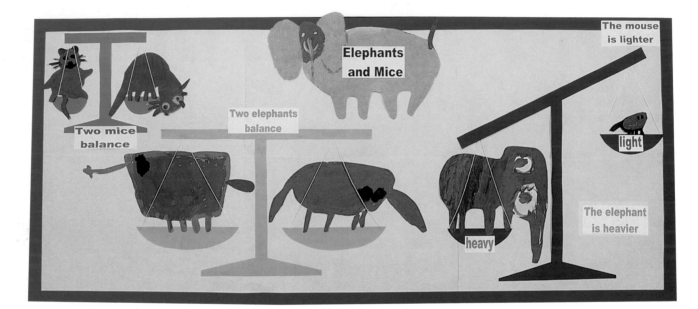

Elephants and Mice (pages 36–37)

First published in 2004 by Belair Publications.

Apex Business Centre, Boscombe Road, Dunstable, LU5 4RL.
Email: folens@folens.com

Katharine Newall hereby asserts her moral right to be identified as the author of this work in accordance with the Copyright, Designs and Patents Act 1988.

Commissioning editor: Zoë Nichols
Design: Philippa Jarvis
Cover design: Martin Cross

Editors: Emma Thomas and Alison MacTier
Illustrations: Sara Silcock – Linda Rogers Associates
Photography: Roger Brown

Permissions:
Page 22: Girl and Lollipop Lady © Angela Hampton Family Life Picture Library
Page 24: Honeycomb on a glass plate/MAXIMILIAN STOCK © The Anthony Blake Photo Library
Page 26: Scarlet, Blue and White Quilt © Jacqui Hurst/CORBIS
Page 50: Six Matryoshka Dolls © Trip/H Rogers
Page 58: Children at Pond © Angela Hampton Family Life Picture Library
Page 58: Boy Mezmerized By Hanukkah © Owen Franken/CORBIS
Page 62: Girl & Dandelion Clock © Angela Hampton Family Life Picture Library

© 2004 Folens on behalf of the author.

British Library Cataloguing in Publication Data. A catalogue record for this publication is available from the British Library.

ISBN 0 94788 270-7

Contents

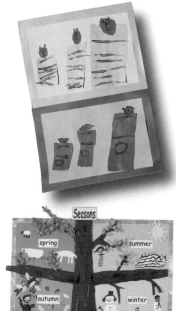

Our balloon is made from willow. We covered it with cling film and then stuck tissue paper over it. Can you peep inside?

Introduction

The aim of this series is to provide resource material covering all the main areas of young children's learning. Each book is a 64-page full colour resource, designed specifically for educators, which provides practical 'hands on' activities suitable for working with three- to five-year-olds. These activities also provide a variety of starting points to encourage and promote creative play.

Written by professionals working in early years education, each book is organised into popular themes providing ideas to develop the linguistic, mathematical, scientific, creative, environmental, personal and social areas of learning. The key learning intentions are provided for each theme.

Full colour photography offers ideas and inspiration for presenting and developing children's individual work with creative ideas for display. An additional feature of each book is the 'Home Links' section. This provides extension ideas and activities for parents to develop the theme at home. A further feature of *Shape, Space and Measures* is the inclusion of 'Free Play' activities that can be set up in the room and accessed by the children independently.

This book is designed to give early years teachers practical, workable activities, which cover the main areas of the early learning goals in Mathematics for *Shape, Space and Measures*. Young children require stimulating activities to develop all aspects of their education. This book provides ideas for such activities as well as creative display suggestions that turn any Early Years Unit into a bright and exciting learning zone.

Mathematics is not just about numbers. The activities in *Shape, Space and Measures* inspire children to find out more about everyday shapes around them, to look for patterns, to begin to appreciate space and how it can be filled, and to explore how items can be measured.

Games, activities and creative suggestions provide a lead into each theme to spark the children's interest. Young children love to explore. The suggestions for follow-up activities should excite the children and develop their learning – often without them realising! Use as many different resources as there are available and introduce the children to the widest variety of experiences that you can. Make it fun! Then you will experience the satisfaction of seeing the children enjoying themselves, being enthusiastic and learning new mathematical concepts at the same time.

I hope that you and the children enjoy the activities in this book.

Katharine Newall

Monster Mad

Learning Intentions

- To use language to describe the properties of 2D shapes.

- To recognise and explore the properties of 2D shapes.

- To look for 2D shapes in the environment.

Starting Points

- Using fingers, draw shape properties (points, corners, straight lines, curved lines) in the air, on hands and on each other's backs.

- Draw patterns on a whiteboard using straight lines, curved lines, and zigzags. Feel 2D shapes and discuss their properties. How does the corner, edge or face of the shape feel? What does it look like?

Exploration

- Make a 'shape monster'. Explain that the monster will be made from lots of shapes with different properties. On a large sheet of paper, paint large shapes using straight lines, curvy lines, corners and points. The shapes can be irregular.

- Decorate the shapes with shiny paper and glitter. Cut out and arrange each shape on the wall to create a large 'shape monster'.

- Look at the finished monster and talk to the children about its different properties. Who can see a straight line? Who can see a pointy corner? Label the monster with the different properties.

Free Play

- Print using different shapes on a large sheet of paper. Can the children match the print to the object used to make it?

- Bury 2D shapes in a sandpit for the children to find. Can they match them to a chart on the wall next to the sandpit?

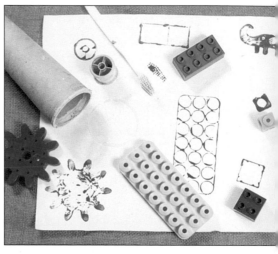

Language and Literacy

- Play a matching game. Draw pairs of simple, identical-shaped monsters on to cards and laminate. Shuffle and share the cards between three to five children. Ask one child to describe a monster, for example: "It is round. It has three legs. It has crosses for eyes." If another child has a matching monster, they should shout "Monster Snap!" and take that card.

- Tell a made-up story along the lines of *We're Going on a Bear Hunt* (published by Walker Books, 1989). The theme should be 'We're Going on a Monster Hunt!' Act out the narrative – for example, swimming in a zigzag pattern across a river full of crocodiles or jumping in a curved arc around a fire-breathing dragon.

Outside

- Provide a bucket, water and brushes for children to 'draw' irregular shapes on the floor.

- Put out large sheets of paper and paint shapes using straight, curved and zigzag lines.

Our World

- Make large 2D shapes from foam, card, wood, fur and bubble wrap. Explore their shape, texture and material. Encourage the children to talk about the shapes and their properties.

- Cut sandwiches into different shapes using cookie cutters. Sit in a circle at snack-time and ask the children to describe the shape of their sandwich before eating it.

Creative Work

- Make simple music notation cards using shapes to represent the different instruments. For example, a circle for a drum and a rectangle for a chime bar. Encourage the children to follow the patterns on the cards to create a piece of music.

- Use different instruments as a stimulus for the children to imagine how different monsters might move. A loud drumbeat could be stomping feet; Indian bells could represent a tiptoeing monster.

- Make monsters by printing with a variety of different-shaped objects.

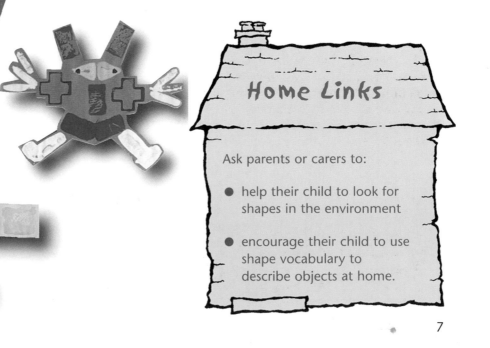

Home Links

Ask parents or carers to:

- help their child to look for shapes in the environment

- encourage their child to use shape vocabulary to describe objects at home.

Model Town

Learning Intentions

- To recognise and explore the properties of 3D shapes.

- To look for 3D shapes in the environment.

Starting Points

- Build a model town from different-shaped building blocks. Who can see a building block shaped like a cube? Repeat, introducing the names of different 3D shapes.

- Sing a shape song to the tune of 'Merrily We Roll Along':

    Shapes, shapes, shapes are everywhere,
    Some are round, some are square.
    Some have curves, some have straight lines,
    Which shapes can you find?

- Which 3D shapes can the children see around the room?

Exploration

- Take a walk outside. What sort of buildings can the children see? Make a pictorial list of other types of buildings, such as a lighthouse or an airport.

- Share books about different types of buildings.

- Make a 3D model town from junk boxes and containers. Include a vertical number line on a very large skyscraper for use in number work.

- Look at the finished town and talk about the different shapes used to build it. Who can see a cylinder, cube, and so on? (Hold up the appropriate shape for the children to see.)

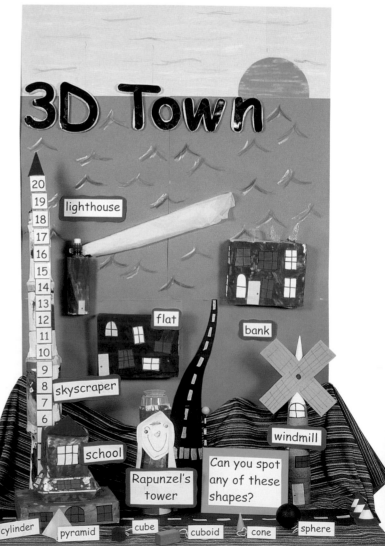

3D Town

lighthouse
flat
bank
skyscraper
windmill
school
Rapunzel's tower
Can you spot any of these shapes?
cylinder   pyramid   cube   cuboid   cone   sphere

Free Play

- Allow the children to construct their own buildings from coloured building blocks. Can they draw their own model for a friend to copy?

- Provide construction kits for the children to make a house for a soft toy.

- Provide different play mats and small world equipment for the children to create their own environments.

Language and Literacy

- Play 'What's Inside the Feely Box?' Sit in a circle with each child holding a different shape. Inside the feely box should be shapes matching those that the children are holding. Volunteers can then reach inside the box, feel a shape and describe it. The children should look at their shape and decide which one is being described.

- At the end of a session, ask the children to share any models they have made. Encourage them to talk about the shapes in their models.

- Tell the story of Little Red Riding Hood. Create a 3D map of her journey through the woods, including Red Riding Hood's house and Granny's cottage. The characters can be drawn, cut out and mounted on boxes, tubes or other 3D shapes.

Our World

- Freeze water in different-shaped containers such as a plastic bottle with the top chopped off, ice cube trays and a balloon. Add the ice shapes to the water tray for the children to explore. Talk about what happens to the shapes during the course of the session.

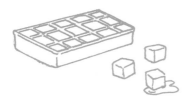

- Build two walls using wooden or plastic bricks, one with overlapping bricks and one with columns of bricks. Roll a soft ball at the two walls. What do the children notice? (The wall with columns of bricks should fall down faster.)

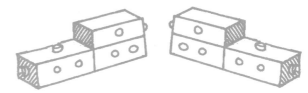

- Talk about why bricks are cuboid and not spherical. Try building a wall using different 3D shapes.

- Give each child a 3D shape to hold. Take a walk and ask them to spot anything in the local environment that matches their shape.

- Provide a smooth ramp to allow the children to explore which shapes roll and which slide. Place the shapes in sorting rings accordingly.

These slide

These roll and slide

These roll

Outside

- Provide large plastic bricks and build a garage for one of the tricycles.

- Find out who can build the tallest skyscraper from plastic building blocks.

- Construct dens from a selection of large cardboard boxes and blankets.

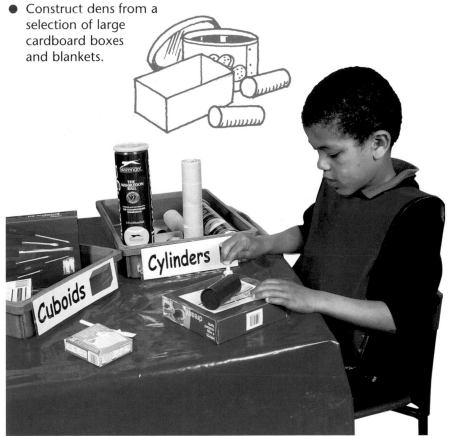

Creative Work

- Sort junk boxes, containers and tubes into labelled baskets. Build 3D models using the sorted material. Alternatively, each child could choose a single basket – for example, the cuboid basket – and find out what they can build using the shapes inside it.

- Print with 3D shapes. Does the print look the same on each side of the shape?

- Use air-drying clay to mould regular and irregular 3D shapes. Once dry, paint the clay models and use to promote discussion about their properties.
  Note: A mixture of PVA glue and water produces a shiny finish once the children have painted their models.

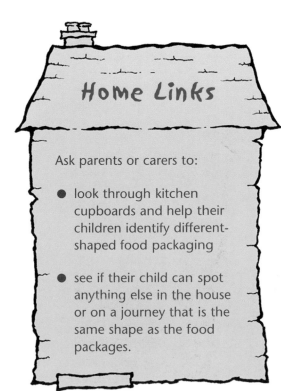

Home Links

Ask parents or carers to:

- look through kitchen cupboards and help their children identify different-shaped food packaging

- see if their child can spot anything else in the house or on a journey that is the same shape as the food packages.

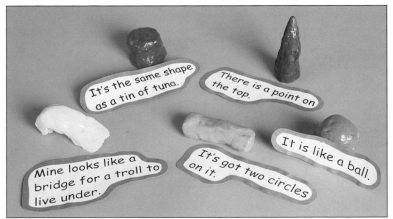

It's the same shape as a tin of tuna.

There is a point on the top.

Mine looks like a bridge for a troll to live under.

It's got two circles on it.

It is like a ball.

What's Your Name?

Starting Points

- Put two matching sets of 2D and 3D shapes on separate trays. Ask the children to look at the shapes and then close their eyes.

- Take a shape from one of the trays and ask the children to work out which one is missing. Can they show you the shape without a matching partner? Do they know its name?

Exploration

- Hold up two shapes (a square and a triangle). Encourage the children to describe the similarities and differences. For example, they are both flat shapes and they have straight sides, but one has three sides and the other has four.

- Collect examples of 2D shapes and sort them on to labelled shape mats. Add to the collection as different shapes are found.

- Create a 3D shape display using open-fronted boxes. Suspend examples of the shapes inside the boxes. Encourage the children to add objects to the display in the appropriate sections.

Free Play

- Put out shape dominoes and encourage children to play matching games.

- Paint different shapes on to the bottom of some plastic ducks with hooks (or attach shapes to the ducks with adhesive tape). If your ducks do not have hooks, an elastic band can be placed around their necks with a paper clip to act as a hook. Fix matching shapes to a set of buckets. The children hook a duck and then place it in the matching shape bucket.

- Provide 2D shape templates (with the shape cut out in the middle) for the children to create pictures with.

Language and Literacy

- Play 'What's Inside the Mystery Bag?' Arrange the children in a circle. Place a selection of 2D and 3D shapes in the middle. From an identical set of shapes, add one shape to the bag without the children seeing. Pass the bag around to music. When the music stops, the child should feel inside the bag and try to match the shape with one in the middle.

- Photocopy some shapes on to card. Draw two small finger holes on the shapes so that they can be turned into puppets. Show the children how to cut the holes out safely. Draw on a face and write its name (for example, Square). Set up a small theatre where the children can play with their puppets.

Our World

- Use shape cutters to make different-shaped biscuits. At snack time, talk about the properties of the shapes before eating the biscuits.

- Put a selection of regular 3D shapes in the water tray. Discover which objects float and which sink.

- Look at a packet of jelly. What shape are the blocks? What happens when hot water is added? Pour the jelly into different moulds – using traditional jelly moulds and some geometric shape moulds. Discuss the different shapes when the jellies have set.

⚠ **Note:** Take care when using hot water near the children.

- Provide play dough and shape cutters. Can the children match play dough shapes to plastic shapes (or laminated cut-out shapes) left on the same table?

14

Outside

- Cut out some large, card stepping stones in different shapes and laminate them. Arrange the shapes as a pathway across 'a river full of dangerous crocodiles'. Can the children cross the river safely by only stepping on? Change the safe shape after each turn.

- Build '3D dens' using climbing equipment and blankets. A tepee could be built from poles and a blanket, or some stretchy cylinders might be available for children to crawl through. What shapes can the children see when they are inside the dens looking out towards the doorway?

- Provide a selection of different construction kits. Experiment and make regular and irregular 3D shapes using the kits.

- Make a mobile of 2D shapes. Cut out shapes from pieces of coloured card. Hole punch the shapes and tie a string through the hole. Attach the shapes to the mobile.

Creative Work

- Cut out large 2D shapes and provide magazines and catalogues. Encourage the children to search for 2D shapes in the catalogues. Cut these out and glue to the appropriate 2D shape.

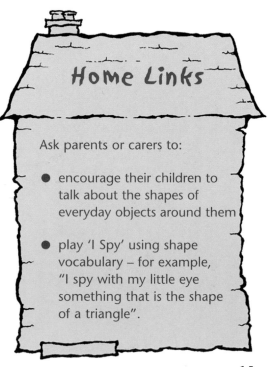

Home Links

Ask parents or carers to:

- encourage their children to talk about the shapes of everyday objects around them

- play 'I Spy' using shape vocabulary – for example, "I spy with my little eye something that is the shape of a triangle".

Bugs Alive!

Starting Points

● Look at pictures of butterflies and other insects and talk about how they are symmetrical. Are people symmetrical? Look at each other. Is there any difference between their left and right sides?

Exploration

● Paint symmetrical bugs and flowers. Fold a piece of paper in half and open it out again. Paint half of the bug on one side of the centre-line and then fold the paper over. Use a roller to ensure that the paper is properly pressed down. Open to reveal a symmetrical bug.

● Include the bugs and flowers in a symmetrical garden display.

Free Play

● Provide plastic mirrors and shapes. Children can make a pattern with the plastic shapes and then use a mirror to investigate the variety of possible reflections.

● Provide play mats with half a face, a house or a ladybird. Place a mirror along the line of symmetry to produce the whole image.

- Print out symmetrical pictures of bugs and beetles from the Internet. Laminate and cut in half. Match the correct halves together to make a complete bug.

- Provide role-play equipment (fairy wings and capes) for the children to re-enact the life cycle of a butterfly.

Language and Literacy

- Provide books and posters about butterflies, insects and flowers for the children to share with each other.

- Make up a story about a butterfly which lost its spots and stripes. Draw a large butterfly with its wings open on a whiteboard. As you tell the story, ask a child to add the spots or stripes to make the butterfly symmetrical. Leave butterfly-shaped pieces of paper in the writing area for the children to use in the same way, working with a partner.

- Look at some capital letters, for example: 'C' for caterpillar and 'I' for insect. Show how both halves look the same when these letters are folded in half. ('I' can be folded both vertically and horizontally.) Can the children find any more letters or numbers that are symmetrical?

- Look at regular 2D shapes. Are they symmetrical? Draw lines across some examples to show that they are symmetrical.

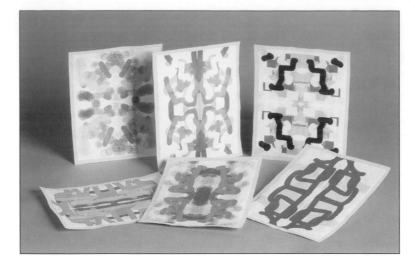

Our World

- Go on a nature walk to look at flowers and insects. Use a pooter to collect a few insects and bring them back to the Early Years Unit to observe. Are the insects symmetrical? Emphasise the importance of always returning the creatures to their natural environment after the session.

⚠ **Note:** Ensure that the pooter tube is covered with muslin to avoid ingesting any insects!

- Use a computer 'Paint' package with a reflection tool. Produce symmetrical pictures. Print out the images and provide plastic mirrors so that the children can experiment with the line of symmetry.

- Bake butterfly buns using a simple sponge mixture. When each bun is cold, cut a slice from the top and halve it to make two wings. Ice with butter cream and add the wings and cake decorations in a symmetrical pattern for the eyes and body of the butterfly.

- Provide plastic butterflies, caterpillars, insects, and plastic or silk flowers for the children to create their own insect garden.

Outside

- Grow flowers in a hanging basket or window-box. Look at the symmetry in flowers, leaves and any insects that come to visit.

- On grass or a soft surface, use a scarf to loosely join two of the children's legs together as if they were in a three-legged race. Can they coordinate their leg movements to walk around? They will be moving like a strange symmetrical insect.

18

Creative Work

- Make hand-printed butterfly puppets. Each child should place both hands, thumbs touching, in ready-mixed paint and print on to a piece of card. For the tail, turn the card 180° and repeat the handprints using a different colour. Fold the finished butterfly in half and add small loops at the back for a child's thumb and finger. By bringing their finger and thumb together, they can make the butterfly's wings flap.

- Make 'stained-glass' butterflies. Fold two pieces of greaseproof paper in half (one inside the other). Draw a butterfly wing using the folded edge as a centre line. Provide pictures of butterflies for the children to refer to. Cut out the butterfly wings and open them to reveal the whole butterfly. Remove one piece of greaseproof paper. Encourage the children to place shavings of wax crayons or candle wax on the butterfly's wings in a symmetrical pattern. Replace the top piece of greaseproof paper and iron over it. This will melt the wax joining the two pieces of paper. Pieces of pipe cleaner or straw can be glued on as antennae.

⚠ **Note:** Allow the children to watch what happens at a safe distance. Keep the iron flex out of reach.

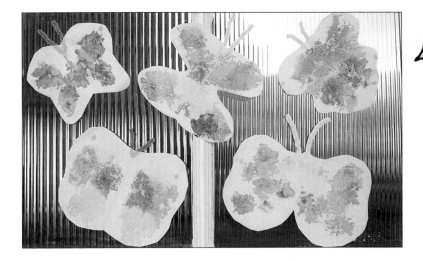

- Pair up the children so that they face each other. One child should lead and move a part of their body. Their partner has to pretend to be a mirror and copy them exactly. Ask one child to move like an insect, caterpillar or butterfly. Their partner should mirror their actions.

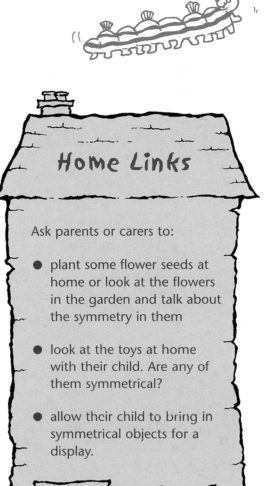

Home Links

Ask parents or carers to:

- plant some flower seeds at home or look at the flowers in the garden and talk about the symmetry in them

- look at the toys at home with their child. Are any of them symmetrical?

- allow their child to bring in symmetrical objects for a display.

Follow Me!

Learning Intentions

- To learn positional language.

- To follow instructions.

Starting Points

- Ask one of the children to be a robot. Provide a robot mask or helmet. Explain that the robot cannot move by itself but has to be given instructions.

- Give instructions to the robot. For example: "Turn to face the door. Walk forward three steps. Bend down and pick up the pencil. Bring the pencil to me." Allow the children to give instructions to the robot.

Exploration

- Introduce a programmable floor turtle to the children. Explain that it cannot move unless it is given instructions. Teach the children how to give the turtle instructions to move forwards and backwards.

- Allow them to estimate distances and make the turtle park in an upturned cardboard box (its home). Some children may be able to program the turtle to turn.

- To help children to learn the difference between left and right, ask them to hold out their hands with their palms down. The thumb and fingers on the left hand form an 'L' shape.

Free Play

- Provide construction kits with simple plans or pictures of objects to build. Can the children copy the plans?

- Put out a snakes and ladders game. This will reinforce counting skills and the children's understanding of 'up' (the ladders) and 'down' (the snakes).

- Make a 'Pin the Tail on the Donkey' game. One child is blindfolded and the other gives him or her instructions as to where to pin the tail.

Language and Literacy

- Attach a laminated noughts and crosses grid to a wall with pictures of two hands labelled 'left' and 'right' above the grid. Hand out laminated pictures with Blu-tack on the back. Give instructions on where to put each picture. For example: "Put the horse in the middle square." "Stick the chicken above the horse." "Put the pig to the right of the chicken."

- Provide an empty bookcase or mount some shelves at child level. Give the children boxes, tubs, toys and everyday objects. Instruct them where to put the objects. For example: "Put the red box on the top shelf." "Put the blue pencil in the red box." Encourage the children to give each other instructions.

- Play the game 'Simon Says' to encourage the children to listen to instructions.

Our World

- Make some peppermint creams and decorate them to look like a floor turtle. Emphasise the importance of following the recipe instructions in order.

- Ask someone from the school crossing patrol to talk to the children about crossing roads safely. They should emphasise how important it is to cross with an adult, stand a little way from the edge of the curb, looking left and right all of the time. **Remember: STOP, LOOK, LISTEN, THINK**.

- Explain how traffic lights work. Play 'Traffic Lights'. Make three card circles in red, amber and green. Red means stop, amber means run on the spot, and green means run. Call out a colour and show the card for the children to follow. This game can be extended to jumping, hopping and riding tricycles and scooters.

- Find computer software that allows the children to select, drag and drop objects. Encourage the children to work in pairs. One gives instructions, for example: "Put the apple on the table." The other child has to follow the instructions.

Outside

- Play 'Follow My Leader'. One child is the leader and everyone else copies them.

- Set up a mini obstacle course with benches, small climbing equipment, hoops and blankets. Call out instructions to the children: "Walk to the bench with a beanbag on your head. Slide along the bench on your stomach. Jump in three different hoops and then come back to me." Choose a child to give the instructions.

- Provide a police officer's uniform and encourage a child to direct 'traffic' such as go-karts and tricycles.

Creative Work

● Paint snakes and ladders for a large snakes and ladders game. Attach the snakes and ladders to a large number mat and use a large dice.

● Sing 'The Hokey Cokey' and other action songs to reinforce recognition of left and right.

● Make a papier mâché bowl. Write out simple instructions and follow them carefully with the children.

● Varnish when fully dry to give it a glossy appearance. Take photographs after each stage of the process and make an instruction poster.

How to make a bowl

1. Mix up some wallpaper paste.

2. Blow up a balloon and cover half of it with tissue paper soaked in wallpaper paste.

3. Use strips of newspaper to build up layers.

4. Make a loop from card for the base and papier mâché this onto the bowl.

5. Use tissue paper to cover the outside of the bowl.

6. Leave it to dry.

Home Links

Ask parents or carers to:

● involve their child in deciding whether it is safe to cross a road and show them how to stand back from the edge of the curb and keep looking left and right

● do some baking at home with their child, carefully following the recipe instructions in order

● teach their child how to lay the table, emphasising what goes on the right and left.

Changing Shape

Learning Intentions

- To explore tessellation.

- To recognise that some shapes fit together leaving no gaps and others do not.

Starting Points

- Show the children pictures of a real piece of honeycomb.

- What shape are the cells that make up the honeycomb? Are there holes in the honeycomb?

- Talk about the fact that all of the cells fit together without leaving any gaps.

Exploration

- Give the children some hexagonal plastic shapes. Explore fitting the shapes together to look like the honeycomb. Also try this with non-identical shapes. Which ones fit together leaving no gaps?

- Make a bee display. Ask each child to draw around a large hexagonal template and cut it out. Make a bee from a yellow card tube decorated with black paper stripes. Combine the hexagons to form the background to the display.

- Add tissue-paper wings and pipe-cleaner legs. Scrunch up some black tissue paper and wrap an uncrumpled piece of black tissue paper around it to form a head. Glue on eyes. Add the bees to a display.

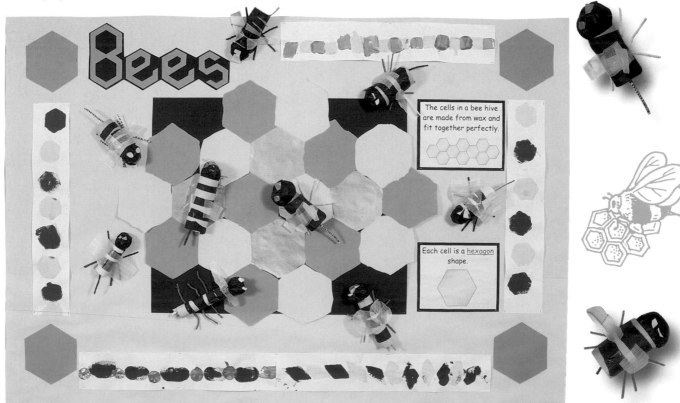

Free Play

- Put small mosaic tiles in the sand tray. Display posters of Roman mosaics next to the sand tray to inspire the children.

- Provide metal nuts for the children to arrange into pictures – they will tessellate perfectly, being hexagonal.

⚠ **Note:** Remind the children not to put small objects in their mouths, ears or noses!

- Provide building blocks to explore how identical shapes can be stacked. Which leave gaps and which do not?

- Put stacking cups into the water tray. Explore how they fit together.

Language and Literacy

- Show the children a selection of M.C. Escher prints that use tessellation. Encourage them to talk about the shapes that have been tessellated together. Do any of them appear to be upside-down or turned around? Does it matter which way up the print is held?

- Cut out similar shapes from cardboard and encourage the children to print their own tessellating picture. When it is dry, share the work with the group.

- Give out magnetic letters and boards. Allow the children to explore whether any of the letters fit together to make patterns.

Our World

- Leave out a collection of zips of different lengths, colours and teeth size to encourage discussion. It is easiest if both ends of the zips are sewn together leaving just the middle part free to open and close. Give the children the opportunity to see how the teeth fit together perfectly, leaving no gaps.

- Provide construction kits with cogs and gears. How do the parts fit together? What happens when one cog is turned? What happens if several cogs are put together?

- Leave out a selection of large nuts, bolts and spanners for the children to explore. How does the spanner work?

- Visit a local supermarket and look at the way that boxes and tins are stacked. Also look at how unusual shaped objects such as fruit are stacked.

- Find pictures of Islamic or Moorish art and architecture, Japanese quilts, Celtic carvings or medieval art, and leave them on display. Examples of these are available on the Internet. Can the children find any tessellating shapes?

- Provide large plastic building blocks. Encourage the children to look carefully at how they join together.

- Put a large mat outside. Can the children arrange themselves on the mat so that it is completely covered? Allow them to explore different ways of covering the mat with their bodies or with a large construction set.

- Cut up an old piece of carpet into a tangram and allow the children to arrange the pieces to produce a picture.

Creative Work

- Photocopy tangrams on to card and cut up to produce pictures from the pieces.

- Make peg crocodiles. Photocopy a crocodile head with very simple zigzag teeth on to card. Cut out the head and along the zigzag teeth, separating the bottom jaw from the top. Give each child a wooden clothes-peg to glue the jaws to the opening end so that they can see the teeth fitting together when the peg is closed. Decorate the crocodile with felt-tip pens.

- Make tiles from air-drying clay. Paint and varnish them when dry with a mixture of PVA glue and water. Place them on a tabletop for the children to arrange into tessellating patterns.

Home Links

Ask parents or carers to:

- look at tiles, laminate floors or bricks around the house, comparing the shapes used and the way they fit together

- look at zips and explore how they and other clothes fasteners such as poppers, Velcro, buttons, belts and laces work

- do jigsaw puzzles with their child, looking at how the pieces fit together perfectly.

Patchwork Patterns

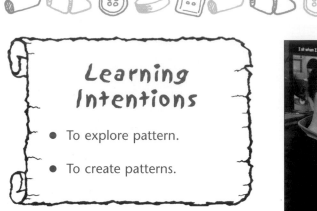

Learning Intentions

- To explore pattern.

- To create patterns.

Starting Points

- Show the children a bead string with a simple repeating pattern on it (yellow, green, yellow, green and so on). Ask them to create a pattern.

- Extend this activity, making the patterns increasingly complex. Depending on how easily the children spot the pattern (white, white, black, black, white, white and so on), extend the pattern to include a sequence using three colours.

- Ask the children to create their own bead patterns.

Exploration

- Create paper weaving with alternating coloured strips of paper. Fold a piece of paper in half and make slits along the folded edge up to a few centimetres from the opposite edge. Once the paper is opened out, strips can be woven in and out of the paper.

- Ensure that the children start one strip by passing it over and the next strip by passing it under. They need to learn the pattern over, under, over, under.

- Print repeating patterns with sponges or other objects to make wallpaper. The paper weaving and printed wrapping-paper sheets can be used to form a colourful chequerboard display.

Free Play

- Prepare long, laminated strips of card showing repeat patterns using 2D shapes. Ask the children to copy and extend these patterns using plastic or wooden shapes.

- Tape several pegboards together to make a large area for children to create their own patterns using the pegs.

- Leave out large egg trays and different coloured buttons or counters. Encourage the children to put the counters into the egg tray to form a pattern.

Language and Literacy

- Show the children fabrics, wallpaper and wrapping paper with simple repeat patterns. Can they see and describe the patterns? These can be left out on display to promote further discussion. Examples could also be placed in the writing area with a variety of drawing materials, for the children to copy and experiment with pattern making.

- Put small trays containing wet sand in the writing area along with a selection of mark-making objects. Encourage the children to make and describe their own patterns.

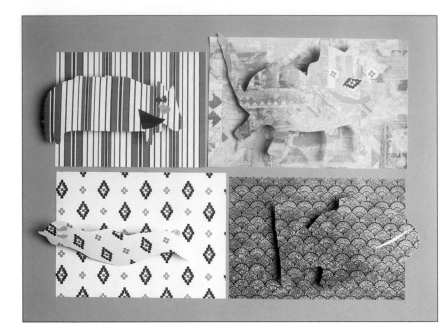

Our World

- Find pictures of different creatures with patterned skins, fur, feathers or scales. Talk about camouflage.

- Make camouflaged creatures. Provide appropriate pieces of wallpaper or wrapping paper for the animal's coat – for example, stripes for a tiger. Draw the animal and cut it out. Stick it on to an identically-patterned piece of wallpaper. Discuss how well it is camouflaged against the background.

- Find examples of patterned clothing from a range of different cultures, such as T-shirts, saris, Ghanaian Kente cloth, Chinese silk jackets. Look carefully at the patterns and allow the children to dress up in the clothes. How do the clothes feel? Would they like to wear them all the time? The clothes could be left in the dressing-up corner.

- Grow cress or mustard in an ice cube tray, forming a chequerboard pattern by placing the seeds in alternate compartments. This is an opportunity for the children to explore what plants need in order to grow. Observe the changes in the cress daily.

Outside

- Provide children with large chalks of different colours. Encourage them to colour the bricks on an external wall to try to form a pattern. Ask the children to help wash the patterns off the wall at the end of the session.

- Look at the patterns on different types of balls (for example, an airflow ball, tennis ball, cricket ball and football). What do the different balls feel like? Put the balls in paint and ask the children to roll them across a large sheet of paper and look at the prints they leave.

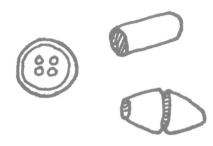

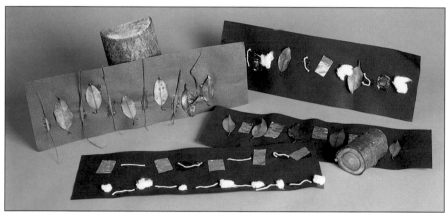

Home Links

Ask parents or carers to:

- talk about patterns on clothing, curtains and wallpaper

- make patterns on a tabletop using cutlery. Can the child continue the pattern?

- grow cress or mustard in a shallow tray containing damp tissue paper. Sprinkle the seeds to form patterns.

Creative Work

- Encourage the children to make repeated patterns with musical instruments. For example: drum, drum, tambourine, drum, drum, tambourine.

- Give the children collage materials (such as milk bottle tops, feathers, leaves, cotton wool and string) to make their own patterns.

- Prepare some simple matchstick patterns drawn on a piece of paper. Give the children another piece of paper, matchsticks and glue to see if they can copy and continue the pattern.

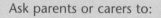

Christmas Capacity

Starting Points

- Hold up different-sized stockings, socks, Christmas bags and boxes. Compare the containers' sizes. Which is the biggest/smallest? Order them according to size.

- Bring in some small oranges. Which stockings do the children think will hold the most and the oranges? Count out the oranges and check. Explain that the biggest stocking has the biggest capacity.

Which box will hold the most oranges?

Which bag will hold the least oranges?

Which stocking will hold the most oranges?

Exploration

- Put up a real Christmas tree or make one using children's handprints mounted at floor level.

- Put a selection of stockings, socks and boxes under the tree with various toys. Allow the children to explore which toys fit into which boxes.

Free Play

● Put a plastic tea set in the water tray for the children to experiment with filling different-sized containers.

● Leave a selection of measuring cylinders, cups and bottles in dry sand mixed with glitter and little strips of tinsel.

● Give each child a yoghurt pot and explore how many different objects they can find to fit into it.

● In the role-play area, provide pretend party food, empty bottles and plastic party cups, plates and hats. Encourage the children play at filling up their cups and plates.

Language and Literacy

● Sit in a large circle. In the middle, place a bowl of water on a tray with various cups and plastic containers. Demonstrate the concepts of 'full' and 'empty' with the water and containers.

● Ask different children to show you an empty cup, a full bottle and so on. Make up a story featuring 'full' and 'empty'. Ask the children to help you tell the story using the props.

● Sing 'There's a Hole In My Bucket'. Prepare a bucket with a hole in it and all the items that are suggested to fix it. Choose different children to use the props and act out the song. Is the bucket full or empty at the end of the song?

33

Our World

● Place sponges and containers in the water tray and explore how much water each sponge can soak up.

● Carry out an experiment to see which balloons have the greatest capacity. Use a balloon pump and count how many pumps it takes to blow up a balloon until it reaches full capacity. Use a visual representation, such as interlocking cubes, to show the number of pumps. Add an extra cube for every pump. Compare the number of cubes to see which balloon held the most air, before letting it out.

⚠ **Note:**
Some children might be afraid of the noise, so it is advisable to give them a warning and ask any nervous children to sit a small distance away.

Christmas Punch

Ingredients
Orange juice
Pineapple juice
Apple juice
Lemon

Instructions
1. Measure orange juice up to the red line. Pour into the bowl.
2. Measure pineapple juice up to the blue line. Pour into the bowl.
3. Measure apple juice up to the green line. Pour into the bowl.
4. Add three slices of lemon.
5. Stir the contents of the bowl. Then enjoy your drink!

● Make Christmas punch. Mark different levels on a measuring cylinder or jug using permanent marker pens and have a recipe ready for the children to follow. For example: Measure orange juice up to the red line. Pour into the bowl. Measure pineapple juice up to the blue line, and so on.

● Make a bird feeder using a pine cone as a Christmas present for the birds. Tie a loop of string to an open pine cone. Mash porridge oats into lard. Allow the children to spoon the mixture over and into the pine cone, filling the gaps. Finally, roll the cone in breadcrumbs and push crushed bird nuts or bird food into the mixture. The feeder can be hung from a tree or bird table.

Outside

- Make up a bubble mixture. Give the children blowers and find out who can blow the biggest bubble. Encourage them to blow slowly. Make hoops from bent coat hangers or wire and dip them into a bowl of bubble mixture to create bigger bubbles.

- A different type of blower can be made using two sheets of paper rolled together to form a cone with an end diameter of about 4–5cm. Trim the end off so that the cone can stand upright. Dip it in the bubble mixture and then blow. It will need a lot of puff but can produce some big bubbles!

Creative Work

- Make stockings from heavy-duty brown paper. Punch holes around the edges and thread with coloured wool. Make a loop to hang the stocking. Decorate with glitter and other trimmings and fill with sweets.

- Provide paper, string, tape, a stapler, glue and pens. Ask each child to design and make their own Christmas bag to hold sweets or candy sticks.

Home Links

Ask parents or carers to:

- encourage their child to notice whether containers are full or empty. For example: "The squash bottle is nearly empty. We need to buy some more."

- put a selection of different plastic bottles and cups in the bath for their child to explore the terms 'full' and 'empty'

- make jelly with their child, involving them in measuring out the water and picking a suitably sized mould to pour it in.

Elephants and Mice

Learning Intentions

- To use language to compare weights.

- To order two objects by weight.

Starting Points

- Ask the children to predict which would be heavier: a hippo or a rat, a house or a tent, a car or a bicycle. Can they predict which would be heaviest? Are all big objects heavy and all small objects light?

- Look at a selection of objects, some heavy and some light. Make sure that some objects are large in size but light, such as an empty plastic bottle or a bag of cotton wool, and that some are small but heavy, such as a paperweight.

- Demonstrate how to pick out two objects, put one in each hand and compare their weights. Leave the objects out for the children to compare weights.

Exploration

- Show a two-pan balance. Explain that when the two pans are balanced, the objects on each side are the same weight. Demonstrate using a selection of fruit. Change the fruit until the pans balance, explaining each choice and its effect.

- Paint elephants and mice to show how two-pan balances work. Show two elephants balancing, two mice balancing, and the elephant tipping the scales against the mouse.

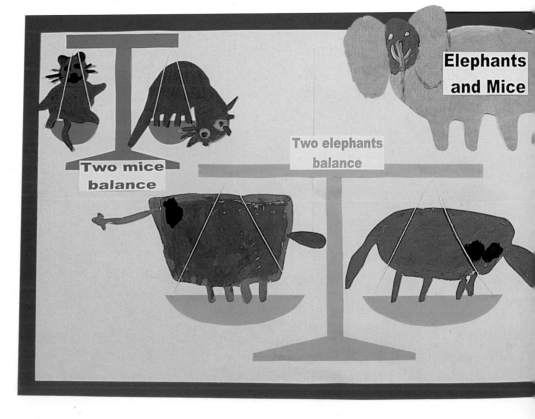

Elephants and Mice

Two mice balance

Two elephants balance

Free Play

- Put toy boats in the water tray with some small objects. Explore how many objects can be loaded into the boats before they sink or capsize.

- Fill three identical opaque containers with different amounts of flour and tape down the lids. Give them to the children to hold and compare by weight. Can they organise them from heaviest to lightest?

- Put a two-pan balance and some scoops in the sand tray. Can the children load the pans with sand so that they balance?

Two mice balance

Language and Literacy

- Provide sheets in the writing area showing unbalanced two-pan balances and a poster illustrating the words 'light' and 'heavy'. Cut out objects from catalogues and glue to the pans to show 'heavy' and 'light'.

The mouse is lighter

light

The elephant is heavier

heavy

- Tell a 'weight' story about someone who goes shopping and buys a different item every day. The children can act out the narrative and show how they would take home (depending on whether it is heavy or light). For example: they could carry an apple but they might have to drag an elephant home or sit it on a big skateboard and push it.

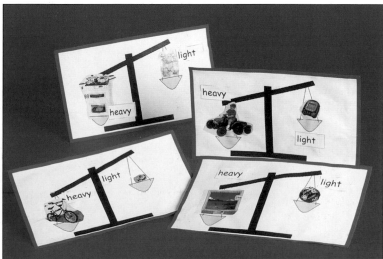

Our World

- Use a set of bathroom scales to weigh all the children. If possible, show the children a set of scales with a needle display and another with a digital display. Explain that these are two different ways of showing weight readings. Who are the heaviest and lightest children? Do any of the children weigh exactly the same?

⚠ **Note:** Take care when dealing with the subject of weight. Some children may have issues in this area.

- Bake flapjack using a two-pan balance to weigh the ingredients. Put the correct weights on one side and ask the children to add ingredients until the pans are balanced.

- Ask parents to provide their child's birth-weight. Compare it with the child's weight now. Is the heaviest baby now the heaviest child? Talk about the way we all grow at different rates.

- Build bridges using construction blocks and rolled-up newspaper and tape. Count the weights that a bridge can hold before it breaks or buckles.

- Buy a helium balloon. Talk about why it rises (because the helium is lighter than air). Tape an interlocking cube to the bottom of some string attached to the balloon. If it still rises, add another cube. Keep adding cubes until the balloon no longer rises.

- Look at pictures of hot-air balloons. Discuss how they work.

38

Outside

- Give the children the opportunity of using a see-saw or a rocker. If there isn't one in the Early Years Unit, use one in a local park. What happens if one person is much heavier than the other? For example, a teacher and a child.

- Make a small see-saw for toys using a plank and some bricks. Tape a cardboard box on each end of the plank and encourage the children to try to make the see-saw balance by adding teddies or dolls to the boxes.

- Give the children a selection of shaped balloons to play with. How long can they keep them up in the air by hitting or kicking them?

Creative Work

- Build a willow balloon. Soak the willow overnight to allow it to bend without snapping. Form hoops (using masking tape to join the ends) and then assemble the hoops to form a spherical shape.

- Wrap cling film around the structure to form a skin. Cover the cling film with glue and then rip pieces of tissue paper and paste them all over the skin. When the glue dries, it will form a hard shell. Hang the balloon in the classroom. Talk about why the balloon is so light, even though it is a large structure.

Our balloon is made from willow. We covered it with cling film and then stuck tissue paper over it. Can you peep inside?

- Make a paper plate see-saw. Fold a paper plate in half and stand it on its curved edge. Draw two people or animals on card, cut them out and glue each to a wooden peg. Explore how to peg the characters on to the see-saw to achieve the best rocking motion.

Home Links

Ask parents or carers to:

- provide their child's birth weight

- allow their child to help weigh out fruit in a supermarket

- involve their child in weighing out ingredients for cooking.

39

How Long?

Learning Intentions

- To use language associated with length and height.

- To order objects by length or height using direct comparison.

- To compare quantities and use language such as *longer* and *tallest*.

Starting Points

- Provide a box full of ribbons of different lengths. Ask two children to pull out ribbons. Whose is the longest? Ask a third child to pull out a ribbon. Where should the third child stand so that the ribbons are in order of length? Ask more children to take out ribbons and order them by length.

Exploration

- Make a display showing flowers of different heights and kites on different length strings and with different length tails.

- Decorate the kites with icing sugar painting. Make a liquid mixture of icing sugar and water. Paint it on to a paper kite and drop spots of paint on to it – this will spread out. Leave to dry.

- Make a tail for the kite from coloured wool and staple tissue-paper bows to it.

- Use garden canes of different lengths to make flowers. Cut leaves from paper and glue them to the stem. For the flower head, cut a circle of card and collage with tissue paper.

Free Play

- Make worms from pink play dough and compare the lengths. Who can roll the longest worm?

- Provide magnetic fishing rods and put small fish with paper clips attached to them in the water tray. Give some of the fishing rods long lines and some short. Which are easier to catch fish?

- Put a plastic map of the world on the floor along with toy aeroplanes. Show the children where their country is and encourage them to fly the aeroplanes around the world, making long and short journeys. Place a globe on the floor with the map so that children can begin to grasp that the Earth is round.

Language and Literacy

- Tell the story of Rapunzel. Did she have long or short hair? Who has the longest and shortest hair in the class?

- In the writing area, put some pieces of paper folded into thirds. Draw three giraffes of different heights, one in each third of the paper. Next to each giraffe, write the appropriate word: 'tall', 'taller' or 'tallest'. This can be displayed on the wall.

Our World

- Plant sunflower seeds. Watch the sunflowers' progress, noting which sunflower is the tallest.

- Discuss tall buildings and structures, such as lighthouses, radio masts, castles and cranes. Is there a reason why they are tall or high up?

- Measure the children and cut a strip of coloured paper the same height as each child. Mount a display at floor level so that the strips form a bar chart. Talk about the children's heights.

- Ask each child to perform a standing long jump (with both feet together and no run up). Cut a thin strip of paper the length of each child's jump and glue it on to his or her height strip on the bar chart. Discuss the results.

- Discuss how a ship's anchor works. Would the anchor need a long or short chain if the ship were in deep water? Allow the children to explore this in the water tray by filling it with water and then giving them string, plastic boats and small weights.

Outside

- Chalk straight and wiggly lines on the ground. Encourage the children to try to find out which is the longest by measuring them using their feet (heel to toe). Which line needs the most feet? Does that mean that it is the longest or the shortest?

- Take the children on to the school field or to a local park and fly a kite. Discuss what happens when more string is unwound.

● Leave out stilts made from pots and strings so that the children can discover how it feels to be taller.

Creative Work

● Provide different length tubes for the children to make towers for Rapunzel. Make ladders from strips of card and matchsticks so that Rapunzel can escape. Draw Rapunzel and glue her to the ladder. Attach long pieces of wool for her hair.

● Use finger-paints to paint caterpillars of varying lengths. Show the children how to alternate colours to produce patterned caterpillars. Use one hand for each colour to avoid mixing the paints. When the paint is dry, draw the caterpillars' faces with felt-tip pens.

Home Links

Ask parents or carers to:

● collect together shoes and boots at home and order them according to their size, the height of the heels, the length of the laces and so on

● measure their child every three months. They should find a place on a wall or roll out a piece of wallpaper to make a chart and mark off the date and height of the child each time.

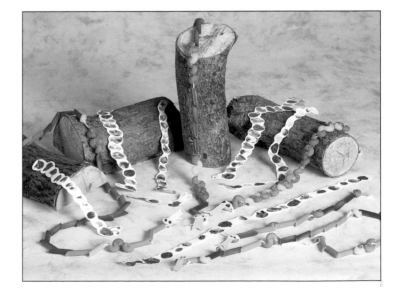

● Make snakes of different lengths from pasta threaded on to string. (The pasta can be sprayed different colours before threading to make the snakes more colourful.) Cut out eyes and a tongue from paper, and glue to the snakes. Hang the snakes up around the Early Years Unit.

43

Thick and Thin

Learning Intentions

- To use language associated with width and thickness.

- To order objects by width or thickness using direct comparison.

- To compare quantities and use vocabulary such as *wider* and *thicker*.

Starting Points

- Find a selection of brushes of different thicknesses (including those used for decorating) and paint lines using them.

- Ask the children to match the lines to the brushes. Use vocabulary such as *thick*, *thin*, *wide*, *narrow*.

Exploration

- Make a giant wall mural using the different brushes. Use the back of a roll of wallpaper or some frieze paper as a background. Paint two or three lines using different width brushes and colours. Lines can be straight, swirly, zigzag and so on. Attach the paintbrushes to the display.

Thick and Thin

Which paintbrush painted which line?

Free Play

- Make some brown play dough. Provide plastic chips or pretend mashed potato (yellow play dough) and ask the children to make sausages, some thick and some thin.

- Leave out twigs or pieces of dowel of the same length but different thickness. Can the children order them by thickness?

- Provide plasticine and a selection of coins. Roll the coins on the plasticine, leaving a track. Which leaves the widest track? Which is the thickest coin?

Language and Literacy

- Put a selection of thick and thin writing materials in the writing area. On alternative days, use chalk and chalkboards, and whiteboard pens and whiteboards. Encourage exploration with the different writing materials.

- Prepare a large poster sheet showing thick, thin, wide and narrow objects. As a group, play a version of 'I spy' but including the words 'thick and thin', for example "I spy a thick object beginning with T".

Our World

- Explore the sausages available from different countries. Provide a selection of sausages for the children to taste. (Check with parents for religious and dietary restrictions.) If possible, try to arrange a visit to a butcher to see how sausages are made.

- Show the children bar codes on food packaging or books. Explain that every bar code is different and that a special computer can work out what the object or book is when the bar code is scanned. Who can find a bar code with lots of thick black lines or lots of thin black lines?

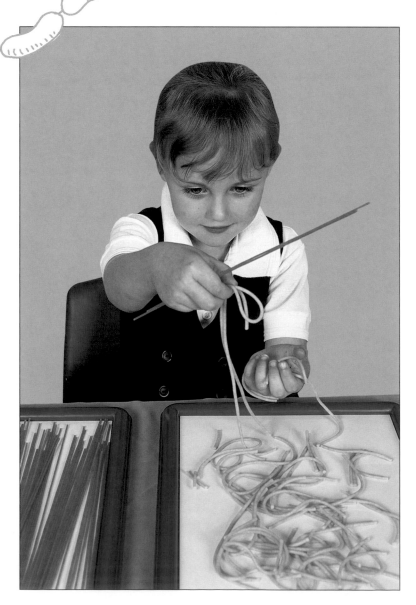

- Provide raw spaghetti, feel what it is like and snap it. Cook some spaghetti in a pan of water. Make sure that the children are a safe distance from the pan. Run the cooked spaghetti under a cold tap to cool it and allow the children to feel it. What has happened to it? How does it feel now? Is it thicker or thinner than raw spaghetti?

- Talk about how a river changes from its source to where it meets the sea. If possible, find a book or sequence of photographs to illustrate this. Can the children order the photographs?

Outside

- Play a 'jumping over a river' game using two skipping ropes. Make the river wider gradually, by moving the skipping ropes further apart. Who can jump the widest river?

Creative Work

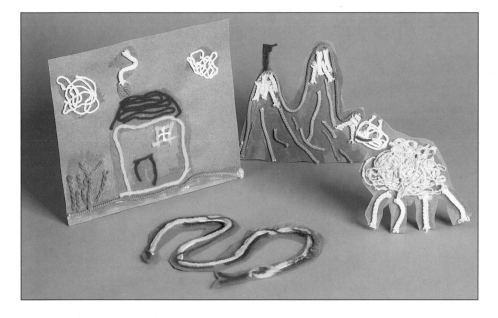

- Provide string, cord, rope and wool of different thicknesses and make collages. Talk about the best type of string for different effects – for example thin for hair, thick for walls, and so on.

- Look at the abstract work of Piet Mondrian (made up of black lines forming wide and narrow rectangles and a few patches of primary colours). Talk about the difference between the wide and narrow rectangles and the use of colour.

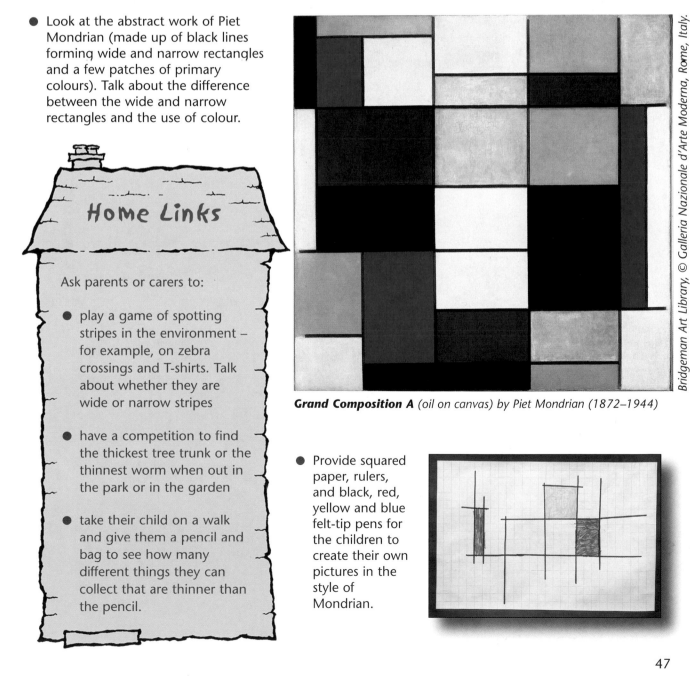

Bridgeman Art Library, © Galleria Nazionale d'Arte Moderna, Rome, Italy.

Grand Composition A (oil on canvas) by Piet Mondrian (1872–1944)

Home Links

Ask parents or carers to:

- play a game of spotting stripes in the environment – for example, on zebra crossings and T-shirts. Talk about whether they are wide or narrow stripes

- have a competition to find the thickest tree trunk or the thinnest worm when out in the park or in the garden

- take their child on a walk and give them a pencil and bag to see how many different things they can collect that are thinner than the pencil.

- Provide squared paper, rulers, and black, red, yellow and blue felt-tip pens for the children to create their own pictures in the style of Mondrian.

Goldilocks and the Three Bears

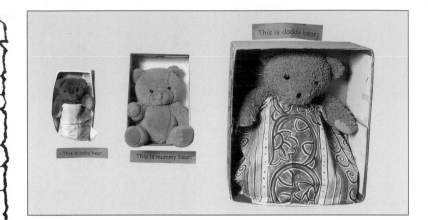

Starting Points

- Tell the story of 'Goldilocks and the Three Bears'. Have a selection of different-sized teddies, bowls, chairs and beds (made from different-sized boxes) and a doll (Goldilocks).

- Act out the story, asking different children to choose bears and the right-sized objects.

Exploration

- Sing When Goldilocks Went to the House of the Bears by Robyn Green (published by Nelson Thornes), using actions to demonstrate the different sizes.

- Set up the role-play area as the bears' house. Encourage the children to act out the story using the different-sized equipment.

Free Play

- Leave out two large trays, one containing dry porridge oats and the other containing cold porridge (made with water rather than milk). Explore how the different mixtures feel and use different-sized containers, scoops and spoons to fill and place in order.

- Provide construction kits to make different-sized caves for different-sized bears.

- Give the children a variety of pastry cutters and play dough. Can the children order the shapes by size?

- String up a washing line with a variety of different-sized socks on it. Can the children order them from largest to smallest?

Language and Literacy

- Find photographs or posters of different types of bears. It would be helpful to attach a picture of a human, drawn to scale, on each photo so that the children can talk about the relative sizes of the bears and compare their size to that of a human. Talk about what real bears eat and where they live.

- Print out vocabulary in a font suitable for each word. Put these words up on the wall in the writing area. The children could collage a family of bears and attach the appropriate word next to each bear.

Our World

- Make porridge with the children. Use language such as 'more' and 'less' when measuring out the ingredients. Talk about how you can add more cold milk at the end to cool the porridge.

- Arrange a visit by a parent and their baby. Look at the baby's clothes. Compare them with the children's clothes. Discuss what and how much the baby eats. How have the children changed from when they were babies? How will they change as they grow up and become adults?

- Provide pictures of different animals for the children to order by size.

- Use a computer package with a Goldilocks program to drag and drop images to recreate different rooms in the bears' house.

- Look at Russian dolls. How do they fit inside each other? Allow the children to play with the dolls and fit them together correctly. Then order them from largest to smallest.

Outside

- Have a teddy bears' picnic. The children can bring in their teddy and a packed lunch. Ask questions such as: "Who has the biggest apple?" "Who has the most drink left?"

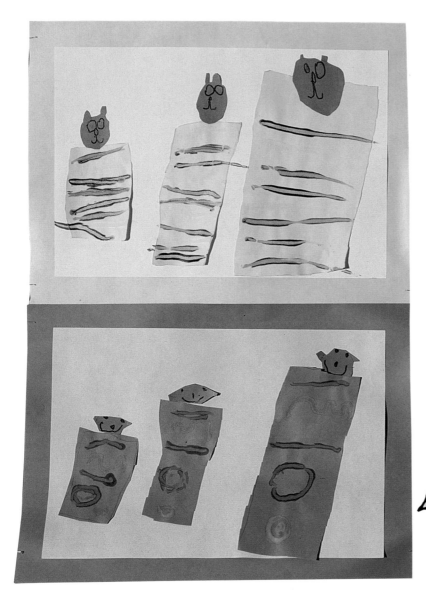

Creative Work

● Make prints with the children's feet. Cut out and order them by size to make a border along a wall. Leave shoes and boots under the display for the children to order by size.

● Create a collage showing the bears in bed. Decorate three different-sized sheets of paper to make the bedcovers. Stick a small, medium or large bear's head at the top of each of the bedcovers.

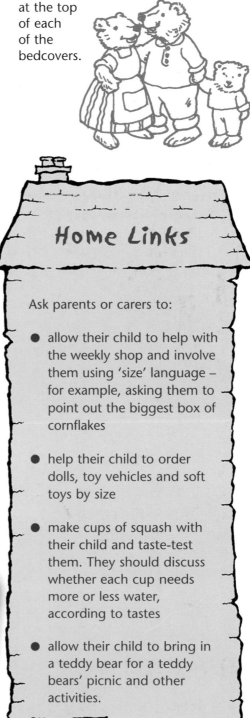

● Make the three bears from air-drying clay. Once the clay has dried, paint the bears and order by size.

● Ask the children to bring in shoeboxes. Cut away one side panel to make a room from the bears' house. Stick old pieces of wallpaper and carpet to the walls and floor. Furniture can be made from modelling straws, pipe cleaners, matchsticks, boxes, pots and cotton reels.

Home Links

Ask parents or carers to:

● allow their child to help with the weekly shop and involve them using 'size' language – for example, asking them to point out the biggest box of cornflakes

● help their child to order dolls, toy vehicles and soft toys by size

● make cups of squash with their child and taste-test them. They should discuss whether each cup needs more or less water, according to tastes

● allow their child to bring in a teddy bear for a teddy bears' picnic and other activities.

51

My Day and My Week

Learning Intentions

- To become familiar with the terms *morning*, *afternoon*, *day* and *night*.

- To learn about landmark times during their day.

- To become familiar with the fact that different things happen on different days.

- To be able to talk about weekday and weekend activities.

Starting Points

- Sing 'Wee Willy Winky' and talk about the rhyme.

- Ask whether it is night-time or daytime when Willy Winky runs around the town. Is it light or dark at night-time? What do we do to get ready for bed? What do we do in the morning when we get up?

- Ask the children to share their news from the weekend. Do they do the same things during the weekend as they do at school?

Exploration

- Divide a large circle into seven sections, one for each day of the week. Mark the weekend in a different colour. Provide pictures of activities the children might do on different days. Ask them to suggest which day the activity should be matched to.

- Make a day and night display. Split a display board in two, leaving half of it for day and half for night.

- Give each child two sheets of paper, one 'coloured and one black. Cut out windows from the black paper and glue yellow tissue paper behind them. On the other piece draw the windows and what can be seen through them in the daytime.

- Paint animals that might be seen during the day and some that come out at night.

- Use marbling inks to decorate small pieces of paper. Paste them on to large cut-outs of a sun and a moon.

Free Play

- Set up a bedroom in the role-play area with clothes such as dressing gowns and slippers. Add a pretend bedside lamp and storybooks for the children to read bedtime stories to each other.

- Pin up a plastic-covered map of the United Kingdom and provide laminated weather symbols. Encourage the children to make up the weather forecast.

Language and Literacy

- Act out the story of Cinderella. What time did Cinderella have to be away from the ball? What happened then? What are the children usually doing at midnight?

- Sing 'Hickory Dickory Dock'. What time did the mouse run down the clock?

- Share rhymes and stories that mention the days of the week, such as: 'Monday's Child', 'Solomon Grundy' or *The Very Hungry Caterpillar* by Eric Carle (published by Puffin).

What do you do at night?

Which animals like to come out at night?

53

What did we eat for breakfast?

What is the most popular breakfast?

How many children ate Frosties?

What did Sophie have for breakfast?

| Weetabix | Cornflakes | Coco-pops | Sugarpuffs | Branflakes | Chocolate trifle | Chocolate flakes | Frosties |

Our World

- Conduct a breakfast survey. Give everyone a square of paper to draw what he or she eats for breakfast. Ask the children to write their name on their paper or scribe it for them. Make a block graph using the squares to show the results and discuss them.

- Talk about light and shadows at night. Create a shadow theatre using a mini-stage with a bedside light behind it. (Make the stage from a cut-away cardboard box with a white sheet or handkerchief as the screen.)

- Make cut-out card puppets mounted on lolly sticks. Investigate whether it has to be dark or light for a shadow theatre to work best.

⚠ **Note:** Ensure that the children know not to touch the bedside light, as it will become very hot.

- Talk about nocturnal animals. Put out pictures of animals to sort into those that appear in daylight and those that come out at night.

- Tell the Christian Creation story, describing what God did on each day.

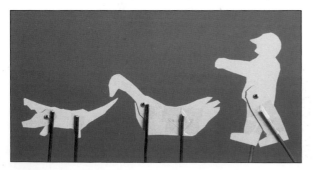

- Set up a tent, rugs and torches as an outside role-play area or use blankets and part of a climbing frame to make a den.

Creative Work

- Sing night-time nursery rhymes such as 'Twinkle, Twinkle, Little Star', and 'Hush-a-bye Baby'.

- Ask the children to design pyjamas featuring their interests. Complete the design by drawing the face, hands and feet and cut it out. This activity can be extended to designing a pillowslip and duvet cover.

Home Links

Ask parents or carers to:

- use the words 'yesterday', 'today' and 'tomorrow' to talk about things their child has done and what they will be doing

- tell their child, when they go to bed, what day tomorrow will be and whether it is a school day or not.

Through the Year

Learning Intentions

- To differentiate between the seasons.

- To talk about what happens at different times during the year.

Starting Points

- Ask the children if they know the names of any of the seasons. Which season is it now? What clues are there to let us know? What will the next season be and what will happen then? Run through the cycle of the seasons.

Exploration

- Make a seasons display. Paint corrugated card brown and make a tree. Use the tree to split a display board into four sections. Use leaves to make prints – green for summer, and red, brown and yellow for autumn. Cut out the prints and add them to the tree. Leave the branches in the winter section bare and use crumpled tissue paper for blossom in the spring section. Behind the tree's branches, attach children's paintings of things they might see in each season – for example, a snowman in winter or a lamb in spring.

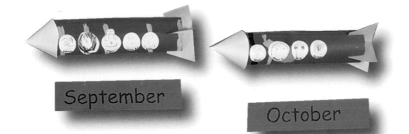

September

October

● Talk about the months of the year. Make rockets labelled with the months of the year and hang across the room in order. Talk about birthday months. The children could draw their face and add it to the appropriate birthday rocket.

Free Play

● Bring in a bag of dressing-up clothes suitable for different times of the year and put it in the role-play area. Make a spinner showing the four seasons. The children should spin it and dress up in clothes appropriate for that season.

● If it has been snowing, bring in some snow and put it in a large trough for the children to build miniature snowmen and igloos. Alternatively, make lots of ice cubes and large blocks of ice and put these in the water tray.

● Squirt suncream into a shallow tray and let the children feel it, write in it and rub it into their hands. Check for allergies with parents and carers first.

Language and Literacy

● Set up the writing area as an office with telephones and notepads. Include diaries, calendars and wallcharts for the children to refer to or write in their appointments.

● Read the story of 'The Ugly Duckling'. Describe the different seasons and how the weather changes. What happens to the duckling throughout the story? This can lead on to a group discussion about how important it is to accept people as they are, not how they look. The children can also act out the story.

Our World

- Describe the life cycle of a frog. If possible, find some frogspawn for the Early Years Unit so that the children can observe the changes, or visit a pond to look at some tadpoles.

⚠ **Note:** Always supervise children by ponds and water.

- Talk about hibernating animals. Why do they hibernate and when? What do other animals do to prepare for winter? Talk about how they migrate, grow a thick coat of fur, store up food and so on.

- Talk about other parts of the world where the climate is constant – for example, the polar regions where it is continually icy or the tropics where it is always hot. What do the people there have to wear? Show photographs.

- Tell the children about religious festivals that occur at different or important times in the year for different faiths – for example, Christmas, Hanukkah, Diwali, Eid and Chinese New Year. Retell stories or celebrate these festivals in an appropriate way. Be creative!

Outside

- Go on nature walks at different times of the year. Encourage the children to say what has changed since the last visit. Talk about deciduous and evergreen trees.

- Play outside on a rainy or snowy day to experience different types of weather. Ensure that the children are properly protected from the elements. Make sure that they are also appropriately dressed on very sunny days, wearing sun hats and suncream.

- Plant window-boxes or hanging baskets with plants that will flower at different times of the year so that the children can observe the changes.

- Make daisy chains in the summer.

Creative Work

- Collage, using seasonal objects such as twigs, bark, leaves and seeds.

- Make calendars that follow the design of the main display. Glue different coloured rectangles for each season on to card. Attach twigs in a cross shape to form a tree. Decorate each section using tissue paper for blossom in spring, leaves cut from coloured paper for summer and autumn, and a cotton wool snowman for winter. Glue a tab calendar beneath the finished piece of work.

- Leave some items that typify the season, such as summer fruits, on an art table with some chalk pastels. Encourage the children to look carefully and try to draw them.

Home Links

Ask parents or carers to:

- make a small vegetable plot for their child, showing them how to tend vegetables at different times of the year. If this is not possible, grow some herbs inside.

Time for Time

Learning Intentions

- To understand that different activities take different amounts of time.

- To use non-standard units to measure time.

Starting Points

- Read *The Time it Took Tom* by Nick Sharratt and Stephen Tucker (published by Scholastic). How long do the children think three seconds is? Is three minutes longer? Three hours? Three years? Ask the children to act out the story pretending that they are Tom.

stop clock

Exploration

- Make a display of different objects that are used as timers – for example a sand timer, a cooking timer, a sundial, clocks (analogue and digital) and a watch.

- Talk about when the timers might be used. Give the children the chance to use some of them by having mini-races. For example: set a cooking timer to two minutes and see who can fill the most lines on a pegboard in that time, or who can thread the most beads on to a string.

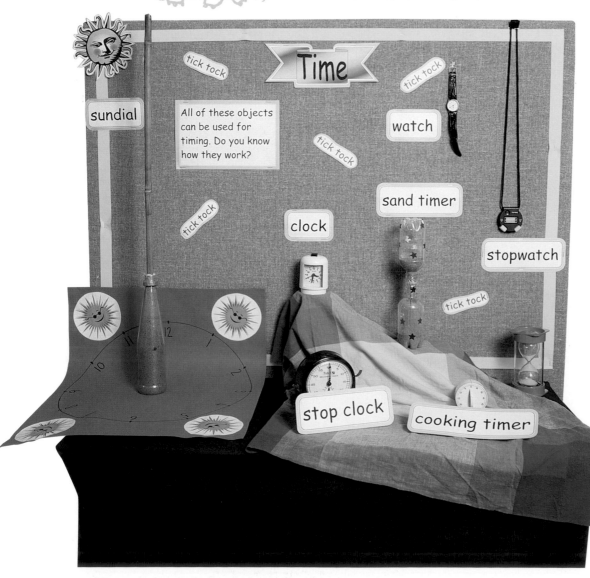

tick tock

Time

tick tock

sundial

All of these objects can be used for timing. Do you know how they work?

tick tock

watch

clock

sand timer

tick tock

stopwatch

tick tock

stop clock

cooking timer

60

Free Play

● Put different-sized funnels and spades in the sand tray. Encourage the children to fill the funnels to find out which takes the longest amount of time to empty.

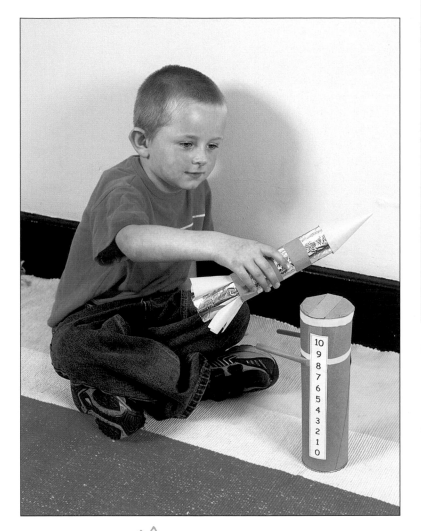

● Put empty plastic bottles of different sizes in the water tray for the children to fill and pour from. Which takes the longest time to empty?

● Provide a 'small world' rocket launch pad. (Rockets can be made from tubes or construction kits if a toy launch pad and rocket are not available.) The children can practise a ten, nine, eight … rocket countdown.

Language and Literacy

● Tell the story of 'The Tortoise and the Hare'. Which animal could run faster? Which won the race? Why?

● Give the children the opportunity to share a story about a journey that they have made. Was it a long journey or a short journey? Was it by foot, car, bus, train, boat or aeroplane?

I went on a plane to Spain. I went over the clouds and I looked down and I saw a boat on the sea. It took a long time to get there. I had dinner on the plane.

Our World

- If it is the right time of year, collect dandelion clocks. Explain to the children that it is a myth that you can tell the time by how many puffs it takes to blow all the seeds off. Talk about why dandelions have seeds attached to little 'parachutes'.

How many school days are there until our trip?

⭐ 10 ⭐ 9 ⭐ 8 ⭐ 7 ⭐ 6
⭐ 5 ⭐ 4 ⭐ 3 ⭐ 2 ⭐ 1

- Use a calendar to count down to an important event for the class – for example, how many days there are until the school trip or the school play.

- Talk about what ice is and what makes it melt. Time how long it takes for two ice cubes to melt, putting one in a glass of hot (but not boiling) water and the other in a glass of cold water.

- Use a sand timer (possibly one that the children have made) and count how many times it has to be turned over before each ice cube melts. Ask the children to help you record this using marks on a tally chart.

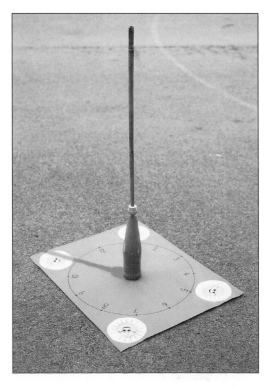

Outside

- Make a sundial by standing a bamboo stick in a plastic bottle weighted with sand. A clock face can be drawn on a large piece of paper with the gnomon (pin) placed in the centre. What do the children notice about where and how long the shadow is? Encourage them to look at the sundial at different times of the day.

- Have a series of sports day races and activities such as a beanbag race or a potato and spoon race. Who is the fastest? How many times can the children bounce a large ball in half a minute?

Creative Work

● Help the children to make their own sand timers by taping two small pop bottles together (with sand inside one of them). A restrictor may be needed where the two bottles are joined – use a cardboard disc with a small hole in the middle. The children can decorate the timer by gluing on a few small stars.

● Sing nursery rhymes and encourage the children to clap out a steady beat. Simple instruments like claves and castanets can also be used. Vary the tempo – what do the children notice about the beat?

● Play some timing games – for example, who can build the tallest tower using linking cubes in the time it takes to sing 'Humpty Dumpty' twice?

Home Links

Ask parents or carers to set their children timed targets, such as:

● getting undressed before the bath is run

● placing all the pieces of the jigsaw in its box before the second hand of the clock gets back to the top. (They will probably have to explain which hand is the second hand.)

● putting their boots on before the count of ten

● boiling an egg using an egg timer. Their child can watch the egg timer and tell them when the egg is ready.

Through the Year (page 56)